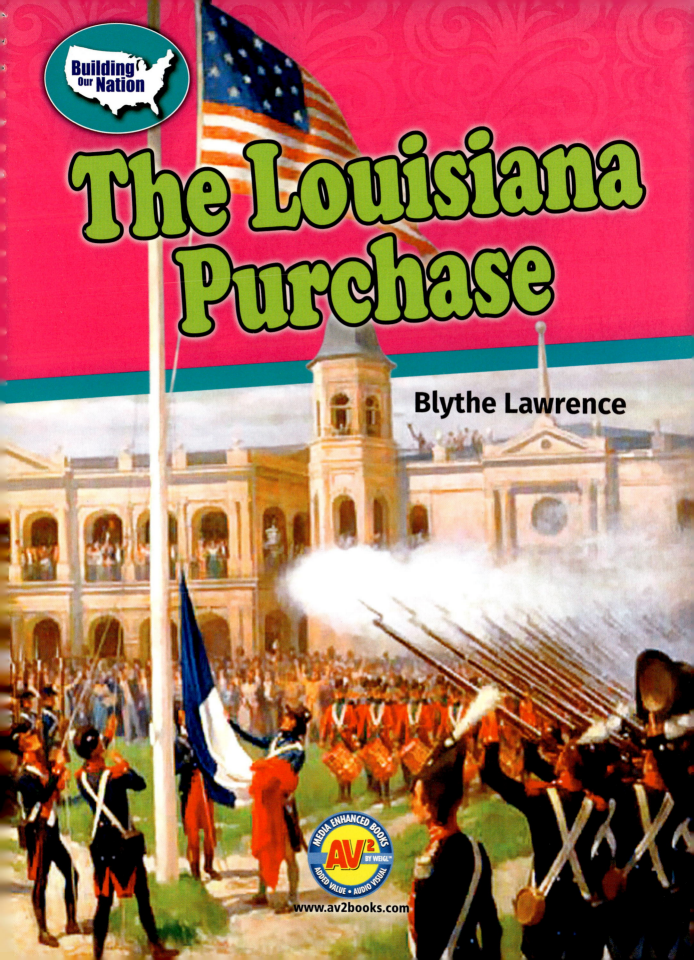

The Louisiana Purchase

Blythe Lawrence

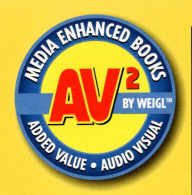

MEDIA ENHANCED BOOKS
AV²
BY WEIGL™
ADDED VALUE • AUDIO VISUAL

AV² provides enriched content that supplements and complements this book. Weigl's AV² books strive to create inspired learning and engage young minds in a total learning experience.

Your AV² Media Enhanced books come alive with...

Audio
Listen to sections of the book read aloud.

Key Words
Study vocabulary, and complete a matching word activity.

Video
Watch informative video clips.

Quizzes
Test your knowledge.

Embedded Weblinks
Gain additional information for research.

Slide Show
View images and captions, and prepare a presentation.

Go to www.av2books.com, and enter this book's unique code.

BOOK CODE

AVU77977

AV² by Weigl brings you media enhanced books that support active learning.

Try This!
Complete activities and hands-on experiments.

... and much, much more!

Published by AV² by Weigl
350 5th Avenue, 59th Floor
New York, NY 10118
Website: www.av2books.com

Library of Congress Cataloging-in-Publication Data

Names: Lawrence, Blythe, author.
Title: The Louisiana Purchase / Blythe Lawrence.
Description: New York, NY : AV2 by Weigl, [2020] | Series: Building our nation | Audience: K-3.
Identifiers: LCCN 2018053430 (print) | LCCN 2018054174 (ebook) | ISBN 9781489698766 (Multi User ebook) |
ISBN 9781489698773 (Single User ebook) | ISBN 9781489698742 (hardcover : alk. paper) | ISBN 9781489698759 (softcover : alk. paper)
Subjects: LCSH: Louisiana Purchase--Juvenile literature. | United States--Territorial expansion--Juvenile literature.
Classification: LCC F372 (ebook) | LCC F372 .L524 2020 (print) | DDC 973.4/6--dc23
LC record available at https://lccn.loc.gov/2018053430

Printed in the United States of America in Brainerd, Minnesota
1 2 3 4 5 6 7 8 9 0   23 22 21 20 19

022019
102318

Project Coordinator: Heather Kissock   Designer: Ana María Vidal

Every reasonable effort has been made to trace ownership and to obtain permission to reprint copyright material. The publishers would be pleased to have any errors or omissions brought to their attention so that they may be corrected in subsequent printings.

Weigl acknowledges Getty Images, Bridgeman Images, Alamy, and iStock as its primary image suppliers for this title.

First published by North Star Editions in 2019.

CONTENTS

Many ships brought goods to and from the city of New Orleans.

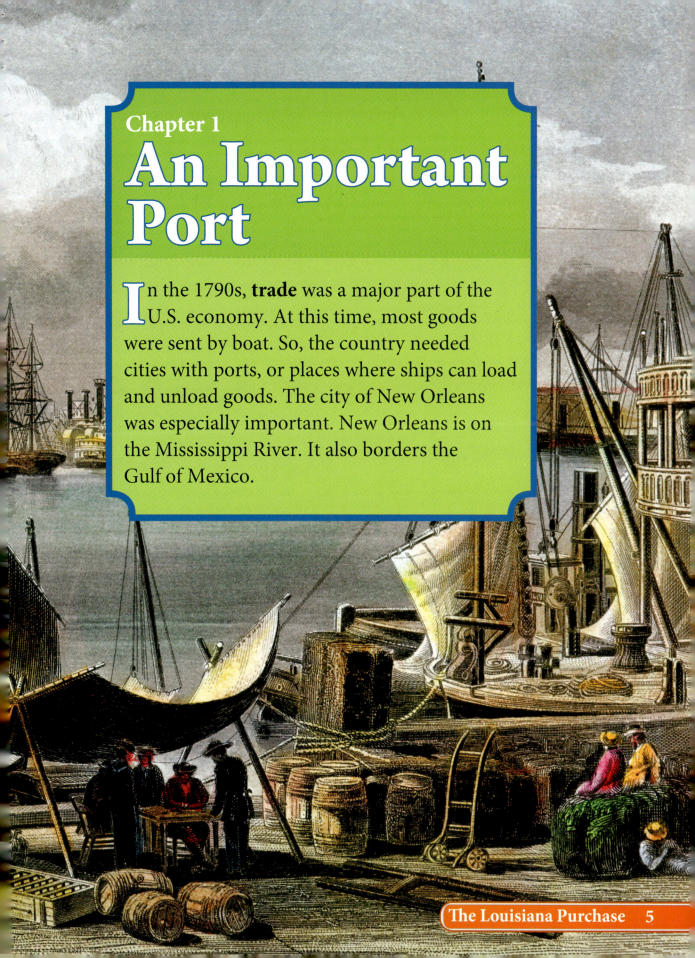

Chapter 1
An Important Port

In the 1790s, **trade** was a major part of the U.S. economy. At this time, most goods were sent by boat. So, the country needed cities with ports, or places where ships can load and unload goods. The city of New Orleans was especially important. New Orleans is on the Mississippi River. It also borders the Gulf of Mexico.

Many farmers and merchants in the United States put their goods on boats. The boats traveled down the Mississippi River. They ended up in New Orleans. From there, some goods could be shipped to other parts of the country. Other goods were sent around the world.

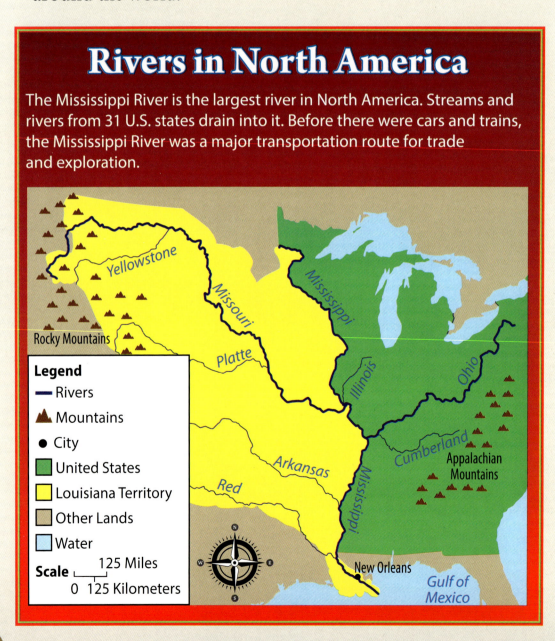

Rivers in North America

The Mississippi River is the largest river in North America. Streams and rivers from 31 U.S. states drain into it. Before there were cars and trains, the Mississippi River was a major transportation route for trade and exploration.

Legend
- ▬ Rivers
- ▲ Mountains
- ● City
- 🟩 United States
- 🟨 Louisiana Territory
- ⬜ Other Lands
- 🟦 Water

Scale 125 Miles
0 125 Kilometers

Rocky Mountains
Yellowstone
Missouri
Platte
Mississippi
Illinois
Ohio
Cumberland
Appalachian Mountains
Arkansas
Red
Mississippi
New Orleans
Gulf of Mexico

However, New Orleans was not part of the United States. It was part of the Louisiana Territory. This vast area of land stretched from the Mississippi River to the Rocky Mountains. And it belonged to Spain.

In 1795, the United States signed a **treaty** with Spain. The treaty allowed U.S. ships to enter New Orleans. However, the treaty expired in 1798, and the Spanish government chose not to renew it. That meant U.S. ships could no longer use the city's port.

In 1800, Spain signed a secret treaty with France. France agreed to give Spain some land in Europe. In return, Spain agreed to give France the Louisiana Territory.

The **first European** to **write** about the Mississippi River was explorer **Hernando de Soto**, in **1541**.

The **Mississippi River** is **2,350 miles** (3,782 kilometers) **long**. That is as long as **322,000 school buses** parked end to end.

Today, **New Orleans** is Louisiana's **largest city**. It is home to about **400,000** people.

U.S. President Thomas Jefferson worried that France would shut the United States out of New Orleans. Without the city's port, U.S. citizens would have a harder time moving their goods. As a result, the United States would lose money. This would create tension between the United States and France. The two countries might even go to war.

Jefferson did not want war. So, early in 1803, he sent James Monroe to France on a special mission. Monroe joined Robert Livingston, the U.S. **ambassador** to France. The two men tried to convince the French to sell New Orleans. The U.S. government was willing to pay as much as $10 million.

Events Leading Up to the Louisiana Purchase

Ownership of the Louisiana Territory went back and forth for much of the late 1700s. It was only when the United States expressed interest that the situation settled.

1762
France gives Louisiana to Spain.

1800
Spain gives Louisiana back to France.

January 1803
The United States offers to buy New Orleans and Florida from France.

James Monroe had been the U.S. ambassador to France when George Washington was president.

April 1803

France agrees to sell the United States the entire Louisiana Territory, including New Orleans. This agreement will double the size of the United States.

October 1803

The U.S. Senate **ratifies** the agreement, known today as the Louisiana Purchase Treaty.

December 1803

A ceremony is held in New Orleans to formally transfer southern Louisiana to the United States. Northern Louisiana is formally transferred in March 1804.

Napoleon Bonaparte became the ruler of France in 1799.

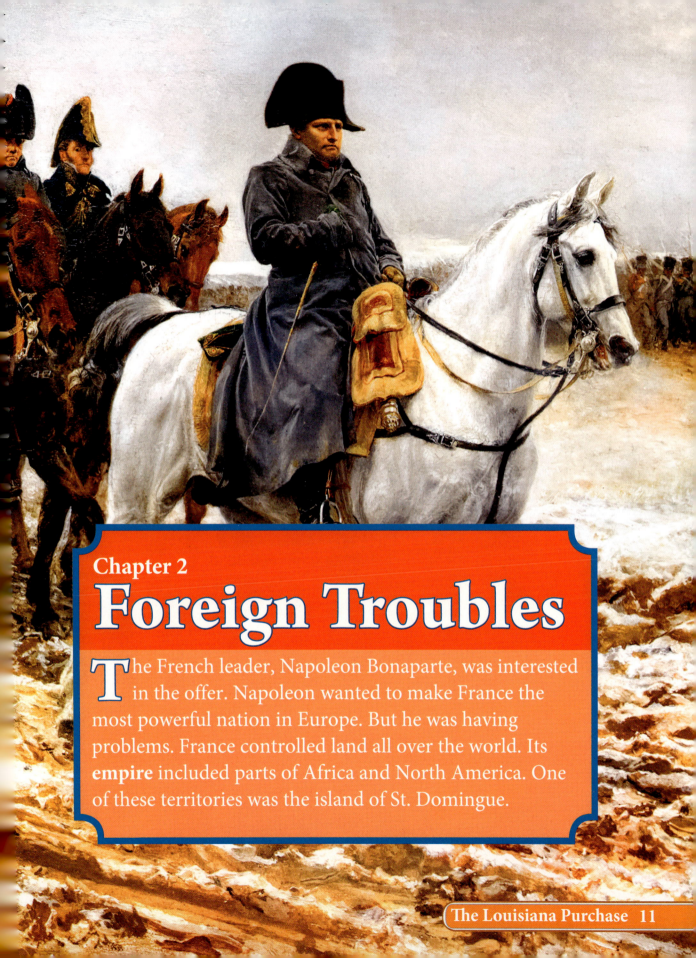

Chapter 2
Foreign Troubles

The French leader, Napoleon Bonaparte, was interested in the offer. Napoleon wanted to make France the most powerful nation in Europe. But he was having problems. France controlled land all over the world. Its **empire** included parts of Africa and North America. One of these territories was the island of St. Domingue.

Known as Haiti today, St. Domingue is in the Caribbean Sea. Enslaved people on this island had begun rebelling in the 1790s. French soldiers were sent to St. Domingue to stop the rebellion. But many soldiers caught yellow fever and died. Others were killed during the fighting.

Meanwhile, Napoleon faced war in Europe. The British and the French had fought for 10 years before signing a peace treaty in 1802. But the peace did not last long. The British declared war on France again in 1803. Napoleon now had a new problem. He needed money to equip his army.

While there was peace, Napoleon had thought North America would be a good place to expand France's power. But the difficulties in St. Domingue and the new war changed his mind. Napoleon realized he needed to focus on Europe. Selling the land in North America would give him money to fight the British.

Robert Livingston encouraged this view. He wrote a pamphlet. And he made sure Napoleon's **ministers** received copies of it. The pamphlet said that keeping the territories in North America would hurt France. Livingston even hinted that the United States might declare war if the two nations could not reach an agreement about New Orleans.

French soldiers were unable to stop a rebellion on the island of St. Domingue.

Napoleon did not want to go to war with the United States. He needed his armies to fight against the British. So, he decided to sell. But Napoleon planned to offer more than just New Orleans. He wanted to sell the entire Louisiana Territory. Napoleon told his finance minister, François Barbé-Marbois, to start **negotiations** with Livingston and Monroe. Together, the three men would work out the details of the sale.

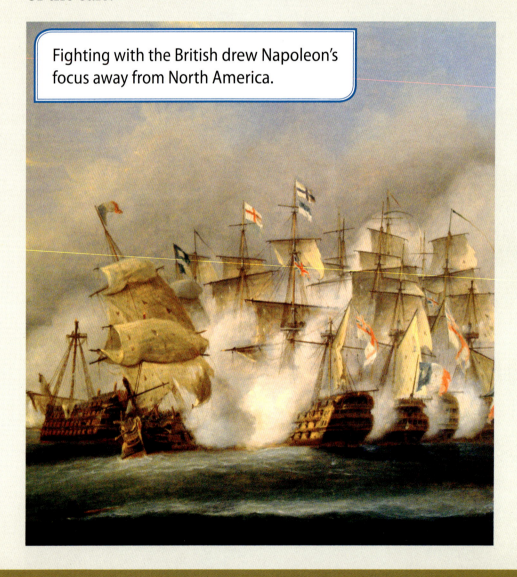

Fighting with the British drew Napoleon's focus away from North America.

The Louisiana Territory

The land that France offered to sell the United States was called the Louisiana Territory. It extended from the Mississippi River in the east to the Rocky Mountains in the west and from New Orleans in the south to what are now the Canadian provinces of Alberta and Saskatchewan in the north.

Legend

- Louisiana Territory
- City
- River
- Rocky Mountains
- United States
- Other Countries
- Water

Scale 250 Miles
0   250 Kilometers

The French offered to sell a large area of land in North America to the United States.

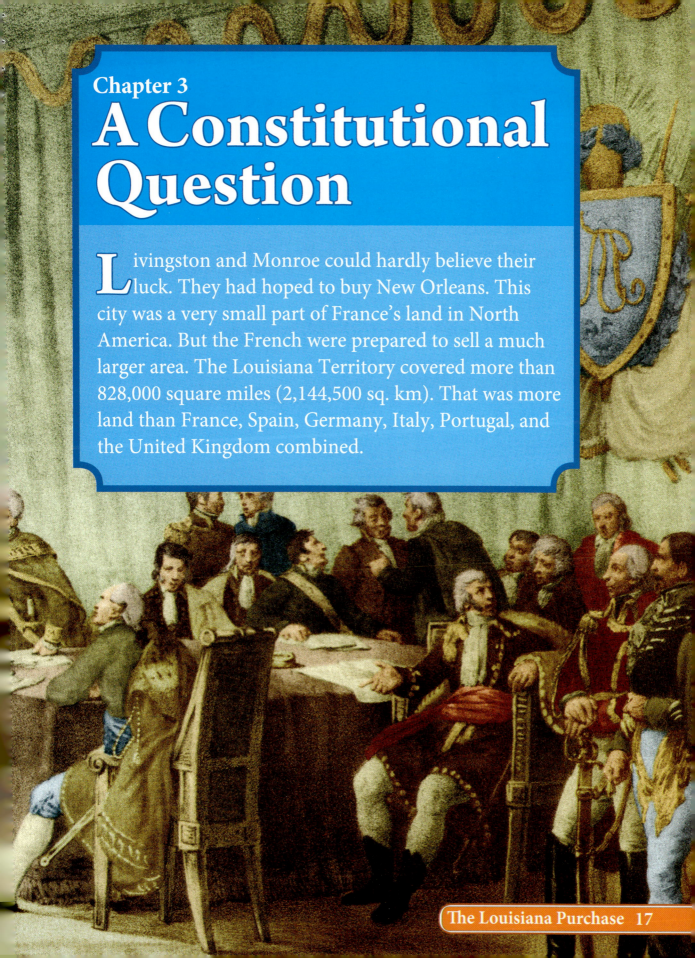

Chapter 3
A Constitutional Question

Livingston and Monroe could hardly believe their luck. They had hoped to buy New Orleans. This city was a very small part of France's land in North America. But the French were prepared to sell a much larger area. The Louisiana Territory covered more than 828,000 square miles (2,144,500 sq. km). That was more land than France, Spain, Germany, Italy, Portugal, and the United Kingdom combined.

Barbé-Marbois, Livingston, and Monroe signed the Louisiana Purchase Treaty in Paris, France.

This land was not empty. Many Native American groups lived there. Even so, France claimed to own the land. And Livingston and Monroe wanted to buy it.

Livingston and Monroe did not have permission to buy the entire Louisiana Territory. However, the territory would nearly double the size of the United States. And it would help the country become more powerful. So, they accepted France's offer.

The Louisiana Purchase Treaty laid out the terms. The United States would pay $15 million for the land. That was an excellent price for so much land. The men signed the treaty on May 2, 1803.

About 8,000 people, not including Native Americans, lived in the Louisiana Territory at the time of the 1803 purchase.

Jefferson was thrilled when he got the news. There was just one problem. Jefferson was not sure he was allowed to approve the deal. As the U.S. president, Jefferson got his power from the U.S. Constitution. That document spells out what the government has the power to do. And the Constitution does not say that the president can buy land.

Jefferson considered the problem carefully. The Constitution did not give the president permission to add land to the country. On the other hand, it did not say the president *couldn't* add land. And the Constitution does give the president power to make treaties.

Jefferson used this fact to come up with his solution. The United States had made a treaty with France, he reasoned. That was within his powers as president. So, Jefferson went ahead with the deal.

The U.S. Constitution explains the role and powers of the federal government.

Thomas Jefferson

People often disagree about how much power the U.S. Constitution gives the government. Constitutionalists believe the government can only do what the Constitution mentions directly. If something is not mentioned, they believe the government cannot do it.

Jefferson usually held this view. But when he approved the Louisiana Purchase Treaty, he went against it. He did something the Constitution did not specifically mention.

Jefferson compared his decision to being a **guardian** of a child. He believed his action would help the young country. "In purchasing an important **adjacent** territory," Jefferson wrote, a guardian does not ask the child for permission. Instead, when the child grows up, the guardian can explain, "I did this for your good."

Jefferson's decision shaped how other leaders thought about the Constitution. They used his decision as an example when trying to figure out what their powers included.

Many U.S. citizens were eager to settle and explore the new land.

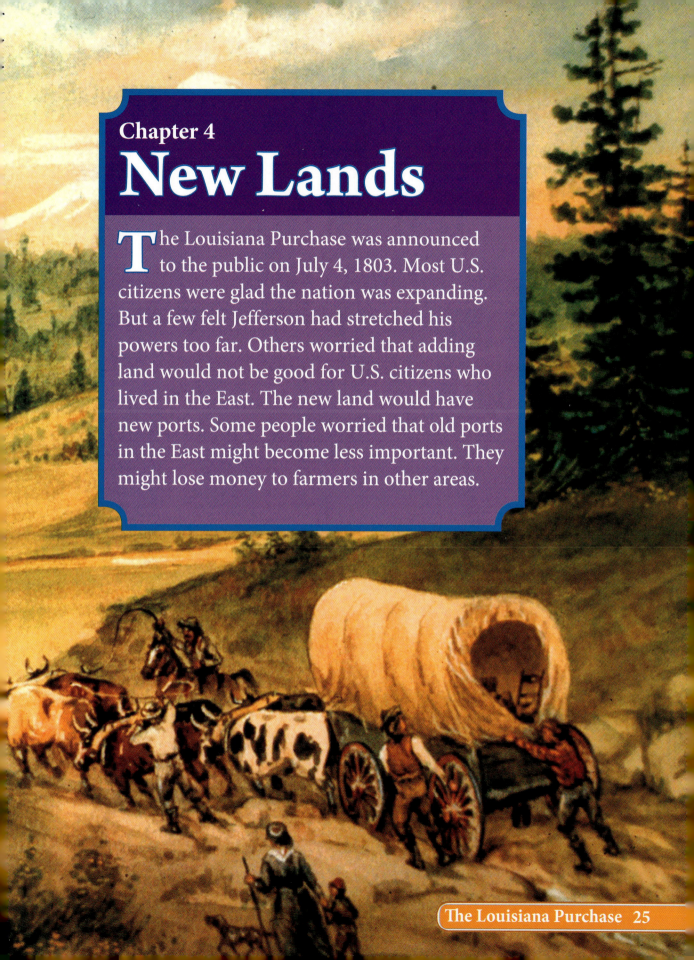

Chapter 4
New Lands

The Louisiana Purchase was announced to the public on July 4, 1803. Most U.S. citizens were glad the nation was expanding. But a few felt Jefferson had stretched his powers too far. Others worried that adding land would not be good for U.S. citizens who lived in the East. The new land would have new ports. Some people worried that old ports in the East might become less important. They might lose money to farmers in other areas.

The purchase was not yet official. All treaties must be approved by the Senate. But Jefferson easily convinced most senators to support the deal. In October 1803, the Senate voted to ratify the treaty. And in December, the Louisiana Territory officially became part of the United States.

The Louisiana Purchase led to many changes. First, it helped trade. U.S. ships could use the port at New Orleans. They did not have to get permission from foreign governments. Their goods could travel freely along the Mississippi River. And ships in New Orleans could send the goods to destinations far and wide.

People often used flatboats to carry cargo down rivers.

Second, U.S. citizens became curious about the West. Few people in the East knew about the terrain or the Native Americans who lived west of the Mississippi. Jefferson sent a group of people to explore this area. Led by Meriwether Lewis and William Clark, the **expedition** began in May 1804. They traveled all the way to the Pacific Ocean and back.

Their journey opened a path for more people to settle in the new lands. By the mid-1800s, many settlers had moved west of the Mississippi River. Some areas had even applied to become states. This led to a heated debate. Should slavery be allowed in the new lands? This debate would continue to grow until the U.S. Civil War (1861–1865).

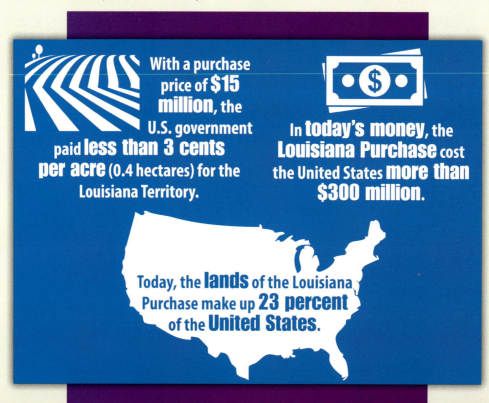

With a purchase price of $15 million, the U.S. government paid less than 3 cents per acre (0.4 hectares) for the Louisiana Territory.

In today's money, the Louisiana Purchase cost the United States more than $300 million.

Today, the lands of the Louisiana Purchase make up 23 percent of the United States.

Settling New States

The land that was part of the Louisiana Purchase eventually became part of 15 new states.

State		Year entered the Union	State		Year entered the Union
Louisiana		April 30, 1812	South Dakota		November 2, 1889
Missouri		August 10, 1821	Montana		November 8, 1889
Arkansas		June 15, 1836	Wyoming		July 10, 1890
Texas		December 29, 1845	Oklahoma		November 16, 1907
Iowa		December 28, 1846	New Mexico		January 6, 1912
Minnesota		May 11, 1858			
Kansas		January 29, 1861			
Nebraska		March 1, 1867			
Colorado		August 1, 1876			
North Dakota		November 2, 1889			

Quiz

1 Who negotiated the Louisiana Purchase for the United States?

2 What city did the United States want when it first started negotiations?

3 Who was the leader of France when the purchase was made?

4 How much land did the Louisiana Territory cover?

5 How much did the United States pay for the Louisiana Territory?

6 When was the purchase agreement signed?

7 Why did Thomas Jefferson hesitate over the Louisiana Purchase?

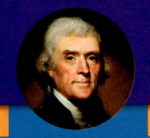

8 How many of today's U.S. states contain land that was acquired through the Louisiana Purchase?

Answer: 1. James Monroe and Robert Livingston **2.** New Orleans **3.** Napoleon Bonaparte **4.** 828,000 square miles (2,144,500 sq. km) **5.** $15 million **6.** May 2, 1803 **7.** He was not sure if the deal followed the U.S. Constitution. **8.** 15

Key Words

adjacent: located near or next to something else

ambassador: an official representative of a country

empire: a group of nations or territories ruled over by a powerful government

expedition: a journey or voyage made with a specific goal in mind

guardian: a person who is responsible for caring for a child

ministers: people who are in charge of sections of the government

negotiations: discussions that take place to reach an agreement

ratifies: gives official approval

trade: the act of buying and selling goods and services in business

treaty: an official agreement between groups

Index

Log on to www.av2books.com

AV[2] by Weigl brings you media enhanced books that support active learning. Go to www.av2books.com, and enter the special code found on page 2 of this book. You will gain access to enriched and enhanced content that supplements and complements this book. Content includes video, audio, weblinks, quizzes, a slide show, and activities.

AV[2] Online Navigation

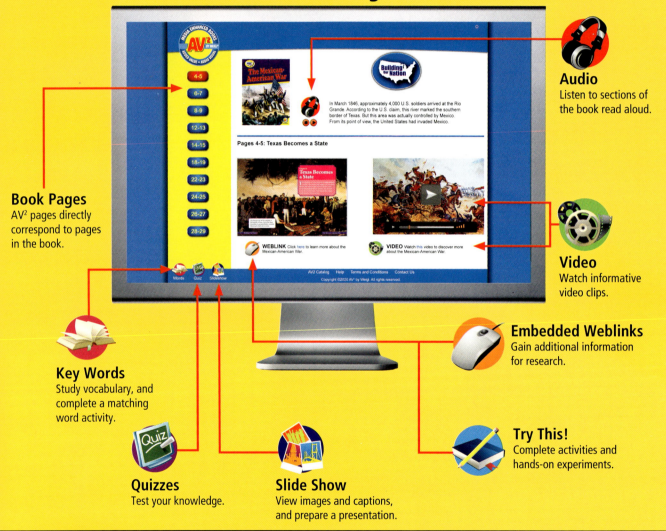

Book Pages
AV[2] pages directly correspond to pages in the book.

Key Words
Study vocabulary, and complete a matching word activity.

Quizzes
Test your knowledge.

Slide Show
View images and captions, and prepare a presentation.

Audio
Listen to sections of the book read aloud.

Video
Watch informative video clips.

Embedded Weblinks
Gain additional information for research.

Try This!
Complete activities and hands-on experiments.

AV[2] was built to bridge the gap between print and digital. We encourage you to tell us what you like and what you want to see in the future.

Sign up to be an AV[2] Ambassador at www.av2books.com/ambassador.

Due to the dynamic nature of the Internet, some of the URLs and activities provided as part of AV[2] by Weigl may have changed or ceased to exist. AV[2] by Weigl accepts no responsibility for any such changes. All media enhanced books are regularly monitored to update addresses and sites in a timely manner. Contact AV[2] by Weigl at 1-866-649-3445 or av2books@weigl.com with any questions, comments, or feedback.